AF415782

KHAYAL

An Intuitive Truth

KHAYAL

An Intuitive Truth

SONIA BATHLA

First published by
Papertowns Publishers
72, Vishwanath Dham Colony,
Niwaru Road, Jhotwara,
Jaipur, 302012

Khayal, An Intuitive Truth
Copyright © Sonia Bathla, 2022

ISBN Print Book – 978-93-91228-78-1

All rights reserved. No part of this book may be reproduced or transmitted in any form or by any means, electronic or mechanical, including photocopying, recording, or by an information storage and retrieval system—except by a reviewer who may quote brief passages in a review to be printed in a magazine, newspaper, or on the Web—without permission in writing from the copyright owner.

Although the author and publisher have made every effort to ensure the accuracy and completeness of information contained in this book, we assume no responsibility for errors, inaccuracies, omissions, or any inconsistencies herein. Any slights on people, places, or organizations are unintentional.

Cover by Neha Agrawal
nehaa.2089@gmail.com

Acknowledgement

One is capable of doing a whole lot, if provided with trust, support, and faith.

Heartfelt gratitude to C, for showing immense faith in me, being my unofficial editor, and always supporting all my decisions for this release.

Thank you PS, for letting me use one of your pieces, just because I loved it so much.

To all the authors that I have grown up reading, which made me have numerous thoughts about their fictional characters. I imagined myself as the characters sometimes, and came up with the poetry in this book.

Many thanks to Paper Towns team, who helped me put my thoughts in a book, especially Manik and Neha, for being so patient with my deliveries. They agreed to multiple modifications, and helped me have this book out today.

And at the end, to myself; Thank You, for believing in yourself, feeling so much without facing all, and working towards fulfilling your dream.

And as everyone else, I can happily strike off a bullet from my bucket list now.

Dedication

Dedicated to all those hearts, that feel a lot.

The Unfolded Emotions

Unknown of the words what to use, but she has to write
something to get off from that flu.

A bad day went down, you probably can say,
an interesting night took a start by a simple 'hey'.

Complete breakdown of emotions and all the thoughts,
some stupid web series untangled all the bloody knots.

The girl who lose everything of her to the roots,
now she's back again to cheer all the loud hoots.

Yeah! She herself looses all her stability at an instant,
but hell man! Look, how well she again gets up and
stand.

She's a reader, a dreamer of her own world,
all the problems get a solution looking at her hair
curled.

What If

Sitting idle, a thought brushed by, what if plants could fly and birds had to stay away from that blue sky.

What if, the world Is all okay with the existence of criminals and intoxication provides all the important minerals.

What if, every job has maximum number of women and all the households are meant to be handled by men.

What if, true love would have been so much easier to find and people use to think from their heart and not their damn mind.

What if, the odds are sincerely honoured and the favours are not something we all have desired.

What if, the world has been all okay with the upside down and it is always the queen who rules the town.

Maa, I'm there

I know I am gone for too long now,
I know I am not there to help you out,
I know I am unable to wipe your tears physically,
But you know na, I love you Mom.

I know it's not so easy without your best friend,
I know it's extreme difficult to find that one perfect hair-
band,
I know it's not easy to spend the day with the absence of the
maid,
Sweet mom, I am sending you some love in the form of new
clothes which are in the trend.

I know people do often show us all their different nature,
I know they will come to us in the near future,
I know it helps when you always have some faith,
Dear mother, don't worry, your daughter is now all mature.

But do you know, how much it takes of you to code,
Do you know, how bore it gets when you have tons of
overload,
Do you know, how much I crave for you every now and
then.
Darling maa, I am eagerly waiting to cycle with you on that
same old road.

नया और पुराना

दुनिया की इस दौर में ज़माना क्यूं बदल गया ,
अपना पराया और पराया अपना कब हो गया।

वो बचपन छूटा वो मासूम सी जिंदगी की ,वो जवानी छूटी ,
कहानी छूटी ।

चला था पाने तरक्की के वो हर एक मुक़ाम को ,
ना जाने इस राह में मेरा अपना अस्तित्व पीछे क्यूं छूट गया।

नई राह में नए लोग मिले पुराने दोस्त कहां, बिछड़ गए ;
ना जाने इस मोड़ पे मुझे अकेला क्यूं वो छोड गए।

अब न वो सपने हैं न उम्मीदें, बस याद है तो पैसा कमाने के
नए नए तरीक़े।

अपनो के लिए जीते-जीते खुद जीना भूल गया;
मरने का सोचकर जीना ही छूट गया...

यूंही कभी बैठे बैठे मैं कुछ सोचता हूं,
पुराने से नए की दौड़ में खुद को खोजता हूं।

फूल की खुशबू लाती थी मेरे चेहरे पर मुस्कान कभी इस ,
नए ज़माने ने तो उस फूल को Air Freshner से बदल
दिया...

उस बचपन की दौड़ ने Temple Run का रूप ले लिया ,
वो चिट्ठियों का सिलसिला भी तो WhatsApp में बदल गया।

क्या कहूं इस नई पीढ़ी से, जब अपने से बड़ों ने भी,
Facebook और Twitter पे अकाउंट खोल लिया ।

ये सब ना जाने कब पीछे छूट गया ,
इस नई जिंदगी ने तो पुराना सब कुछ छीन लिया।

Dilemma

Years ago, months ago, days ago, even hours ago,
I was happy…
I still am, but with some sadness,
Saddening, a bit more with each passing second,
And no, I don't have any reason for it,
I don't have any troubles, no issues, no worries, no
problems, no nothing....
But yes, I'm sadly happy...
I am laughing with tears dropping by my side,
I am loving with some aches in my heart...
I'm forgiving but with an empty soul.
I'm dancing while complaining the sore feet,
I'm spending keeping the calculations in mind,
I'm sleeping with my alarm volume on full,
I'm reading a book keeping count of the pages,
I'm doing everything and yet complaining every
second....
And now here I'm in a dilemma, what if I'm happy and
sadness follows it everywhere or I'm actually sad and so
want to be happy.

ख़्याल

यूंही कहीं बैठी थी मैं कभी कि कुछ ख़्याल आने लगा ;
क्यूं हूं मैं यहां...ये सवाल परेशान करने लगा ,

ऐसा क्या था मुझ मे ;जो जीवन इतना खूबसूरत मिला ,
ऐसा क्या था उनमे की ,जिंदगी होते हुए भी उन्हे मरना ,
...पड़ा

आज पीछे मुड़के देखा तो यादों के समंदर में खो गई ;
फिर एक पल ख्याल आया कि यादें भी होंगी क्या उनके
पास कोई।

माँ ;कुछ और बना के दो न मुझे ,ये खाने का मन नहीं ,
वो कहते हैं तो देदो ना ,रात का बचा हुआ हो ,दीदी ,हमे...

नएनए- से कपड़ो को भी इनकार कर दिया था मैंने ;
उनके बदन पर आधे से नंगे कपड़े देख शर्म से , सिर झुका
लिया था मैंने...

ज़िंदगी ख़ूबसूरत है ;ये माना था मैंने ,
पर अगर उनकी जगह होतीतो शायद इस ज़िंदगी को ,
...कोसा होता मैंने

युं तो नारे लगाये थे हमने कि लड़का लड़की एक समान ;
गरीब को -अमीर ,अच्छा होता की इससे पहले न करते हम
...अस्मान

आज ;बनना तुम ,इंजीनियर ,डॉक्टर ,सबने अपनी राह दी ,
काश कि कोई ये सिखा देता कि सबसे पहले अच्छा
...इंसान बनना तुम

Why Exactly

Why is it always the moon who needs the sun in order to glow?

Why is it always the outrage on the basis of which kindness judged?

Why is it always the girl who has to work her ass off to make the mark in this male-dominated world?

Why is it always the worst to have the realization that good exists?

Why is it always the hate which is strongly demanded for true love to be felt?

Why is it always the negativity which is criticized for the positivity to enter?

Just for once, why can't it be the "wrong" which gets all the praises as in to realize that "right" is right in real.

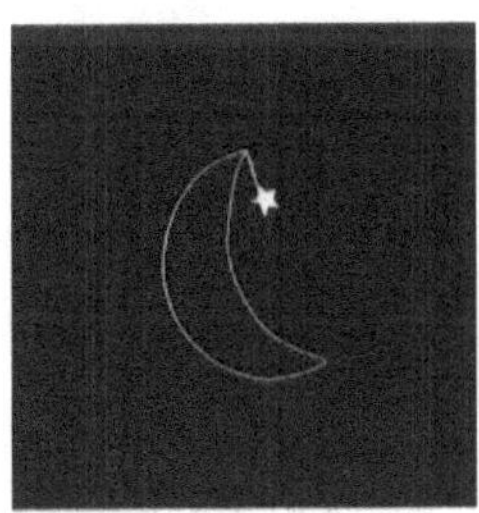

जुदाई

बात थी कुछ और, वजाह तूने कुछ और ही बतायी थी;

अगर छोड़ना ही था मुझे तो क्यूं इतना करीब आई थी;

दिल तूने तोड़ा मेरा, आंख तेरी क्यूं भर आई थी;

मुझे खुद से अलग करने का ख़्याल तेरा, खुद को मुझसे कहां जुदा कर पाई थी।

कह देती नहीं जीना तेरे साथ, खुद की जान क्यूं दे आई थी,

आखिर क्या खता हुई मुझसे यूं कि सजा तू खुद को दे बैठी थी,

अपना नहीं मेरा ख़्याल करती, मेरे जीने की वजह तू मिटा आई थी;

सुना है सच्ची मोहब्बत नहीं होती नसीब सब को, तू नफ़रत भी कहाँ कर पाई थी।

नहीं हूं मैं तेरे लिए, ये यक़ीन तेरा;

लेकिन मेरे लिए सिर्फ तू बनायी गई थी,

मुझे सुधारने की थी जिद तेरी, आदत मेरी कहां बदल पाई थी;

हर बंधन तोड़ने की चाह तेरी, अपनी धड़कन को मुझसे कहां जुदा कर पाई थी।

हर पल नज़र चुराना तेरा, मेरी नज़रों को कहां हटा पाई थी;

मेरी हर ना को हां में बदलने वाली, आज खुद इनकार कर बैठी थी,

गर्व है मुझे मेरे प्यार पे, शायद कुदरत की वो निशानी थी;

अपने से पहले दुसरो का सोचने वाली, शायद जन्नत की वो कोई परी थी।

Not anymore

Today, again, our eyes met,
you saw me and I kept looking into your eyes.
You were wearing my favourite black shirt and I was in
the new white salwar-kameez,
which now I know, got added in your favourite's list.
Yes, I could tell this by the way you kept finding ways
to look at me, midst of all.
You had my favourite coffee again and I looped onto
your favourite song.
You had my favourite soup for lunch and I had watched
your favourite series to bed.
We still enjoy each other's favourite things to self.
But apparently, we are not each other's favourite
person.
Not anymore.

दर्द

चाहती थी मैं कुछ और, हासिल कुछ और ही हुआ;

जिसे दुआ थी मांगी , दर्द उस से ही ज्यादा हुआ।

प्यार न था मुझे उस से; नफ़रत का शिकार वो क्यूं बना;

दिल को ना था दर्द कभी, राहत की वजह वो क्यूं बना।

रोशनी से नफ़रत मुझे, तारों को क्यूं अनदेखा होना पड़ा;

अपने आप से हर पल मुझे, क्यूं इस कदर छुपना पड़ा।

रात का होना, वजूद था मेरे होने का,

उस से फिर मुझे क्यूं बेइंतहां लड़ना पड़ा।

सपनों की दुनिया में था कहीं घर मेरा;

हकीकत के लिए क्यूं मुझे उसे पीछे छोड़ना पड़ा।

इरादा ना था उसे रूलाने का मेरा, न चाहते हुए खुद को
हसाना पड़ा;

झूठ ना था पसंद कभी मुझे, फिर क्यूं ये सच मुझे ही बताना
पड़ा।

काश कोई समझ जाता मुझे यूं, हर किसी को न मुझे अंजान
कहना होता;

पता पूछते हैं लोग हर तरफ , अपना रास्ता मुझे ही बताना
पड़ा।

मिल गया आज मुझे वो, जिसको चाहा मैंने यूं इस तरह;

काश इस खोज में, मुझे खुद को न गवाना पड़ता।

चाहती थी मैं कुछ और, हासिल कुछ और ही हुआ;
जिसे दुआ थी मांगी , दर्द उस से ही ज्यादा हुआ।

Bus Stop

Here, I am standing again, waiting.
at the same old bus stop, crossing my hands around
myself,
thinking of all the good things happened to me;

Like how dear was coffee to me, and the one time that I
had it with extra sugar,
it's not like I haven't given it one more try, but then, it
didn't taste the same.

Like how favourite was that song to me, and one day
you made someone else hear it;
it's not like I haven't heard it anymore again, but now
the words don't mean the same.

Like how much I adore the slow waves of ocean, and
one time I almost drowned in the water,
it's not like I have not visited any ocean or sea again, but
now it did not calm me the same.

And today I am standing here again, at the same old bus
stop, not to pick you up like I always do,
but to say goodbye, to you and your memories.
A mere fact I got to learn that day,
Bus stops are not only the start of an outing;
sometimes, it's the end of the journey, too.

अपने नाम

रात थी अंधेरी, घनी वो शाम;
कोई पूछ गया मुझसे मेरा नाम।

प्रीत में डूबी मैं, दीवानी हो कोई;
दिल पूछ बैठा अब क्या होगा अंजाम।

शम्मा वो भुजी हुई, रोशन ना हो सकी;
कैसे दिखाऊ तुझे, मीत का वो पैग़ाम ।

खुद से लड़ती, टुकड़ो में बिखरी;
पिरोने वाले, देख रहा है ना हाल।

काँटों पर चली मैं, खुशी किसी की;
अपनो ने ही मिटा दिए मेरे अब निशान।

तारा भी टूटा किसी और की चाहत पे;
मेरी खुशी ही कर दी उसने किसी और के नाम।

नफ़रत की ये भाषा, प्यार न बदल सकी;
उसे पाना आज भी है किसी का मुकाम।

सिक्को की खनक अनसूनी हो उठी;
कोई बेच आया उन्हे लिए हाथ में जाम।

दिल के हाल इज़हार ना हो सके;
हर अधूरी कहानी बयान करती ये शाम।

मुट्ठी भी रेत को कैद ना कर सकी;
पंख लगा उड़ गई वो याद।

खुशी ने भी गम को सहारा दे दिया;
अपनी हसी भी कर दी उसने किसी पर कुर्बान।

बारिश की बूंद समा बीघा गई;
पीछे छोड गई, सौंदी खुशबू की छाप ।

हर दर्द की दवा न बन सकी;
तन्हाई में चिपे हैं कई अनकहे जवाब।

सूरज की रोशनी अँधेरा मिटा गई;
प्यार ने कर ली, नफ़रत भी अपने नाम।

Never in Love

I was never in love with you,
I have never been
But yes, I did feel for you,
Why you had to do all that with so keen.

You broke my trust,
I was okay;
But today, you broke me
And you still want to be okay?

We were not lovers
Neither were we friends;
Being more than that to each other
And see, now how did it end.

Hatred is opposite of love
It's said, if you've loved a lot, you'll hate that person a
lot
What should I do now
When we are in love after ending of the hatred slot.

I was never in love with you
I've never been
But I did feel for you
Why you had to do that all with so keen.

जिंदगी से बातचीत

काश जिंदगी धोखा बता के देती, तैयार मैं कुछ खुदको भी रखती;

काश ये कह देती, जीना है तो यूं जी; हसना है तो पहले रोना सीख;

हूं तो जिंदगी तेरी मैं, लेकिन जिएगी तू मुझे किसी और के लिए...

दिए हैं मैंने आँसू तुझे हर पल, मुस्कुरा के ना कर शर्मिंदा अब हर पल...

कोस ले हजारो दफा तू मुझे, बचपन ना लौटा पाउंगी अब कभी तुझे...

क्यूं तारों ने चुना मुझे तेरे लिए, धुंध कहीं कोई राज़ ना छुपा हो इसमे...

जी ले जिस कदर जीना चाहे तू; फिर शायद कभी न मिल पाउं तुझे यूं...

Are you Sure

When we were there, lost all over in each other's eyes;
are you sure we were not in love?

When we were minding each other's choice even in
sartorial stuffs;
are you sure we were not in love?

When slowly, the music queue got the title as "our
playlist";
are you sure we were not in love?

When even a room full of people didn't stop us from
having conversations;
are you sure we were not in love?

When me hating one person made you hate him more
without knowing the reason;
are you sure we were not in love?

When we went out of the box and did any and
everything to make one and another happy;
are you sure we were not in love?

Now when we are avoiding each other, filling our hearts
with extreme hate,
as to not fall for one another;
are you sure we are already not in love?

Getting Over

I am trying to get over you,
Since the first day our eyes met,
from the time I've found your shadow besides mine,
from the second I've realized, my words starts to
fumble while talking to you,
from the minute I lose all my calm and cool, seeing you
standing by,
that moment I acted dumb, asking you to pass the pen
you've borrowed a while,
from the time of ignoring you, if not, then you'll climb
up in my head,
from the time, I got this weird feeling that my hatred
will vanish, if we continued sharing this heated room
between us,
I am trying to get over, even when I am with you,
I am trying to get over you all this while.

ज़िन्दगी

यूंही कभी बैठे-बैठे मैं कुछ सोचता हूं, सवालों की दुनिया में, एक प्रश्न पर अटका हूं...

पूछ बैठता हूं खुद से कि आखिर क्या है जिंदगी, जवाब के लिए खुद को चौराहे पे खड़ा पाता हूं...

अजीब है जिंदगी के किस्से यारों,कभी जीता हुआ भी हार मान लेता है तो कभी हारा हुआ भी जीत जाता है...

हर कदम पे इम्तेहान लेने की ठानती है, हर पल एक नई चुनौती दे जाती है..

हंसते हुए को रूला देती है और रोने वाले को हसना सीखा देती है...

हर कदम पे मुसीबतों से परिचय कराती है, हर वक्त कुछ नया सीखा जाती है...

एक सवाल का जवाब ढूंढो तो सवाल ही बदल देती है, जैसे खुदको किसी पिंजरे में बंद रखती है...

खुल के जीने वाले को मौत के खौफ से रु-ब-रू कराती है और मरने वाले को जीने की वो एक वजह दे जाती है...

वैसे देती वो हमें परिवार का साथ है, लेकिन मुश्किल में तो बेटा भी बाप के खिलाफ है...

बचपन से बुड़ापे तक का समय, बस यूंही बीत जाता है, अपने आप को ढूंढते हुए मौत का वक्त आ जाता है..

आ गया हूं जिंदगी के उस आखिरी पड़ाव पर,

जहां "जिंदगी" का मतलब शायद जीना ही पाया है..

The Same hour

It's 3:02 in the morning,
and yet you're on my mind,
this time not because I miss you,
but with the thought that how much I missed myself in the
process of forgetting you.

It's the same hour,
when we used to talk so much, once;
and this time I'm sitting idle,
but realizing how much I've wasted to continue us with the
missing fourth wheel.

It's the same time in the clock,
when we used to sit in the balcony with our hands crossing
each other's.
and now it's you and me there in the balcony,
but me hugging the cold breeze and you smoking us out in
the harmony.

It's that same time,
when once we were happy to share our sad moments,
and now it seems sad,
even to share our happy stories, we don't have each other as
opponents.

It's that time,
when I miss you as my known,
But again, what to do now,
when you made me realize it's better to love myself being
alone.

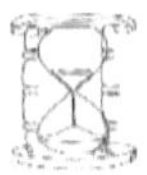

तुम्हारी याद

रात के एक बज के सात मिनट हो रहे हैं,
और हमें अलग हुए पूरे तीन...महिने-
खिड़की के बहार देख रही हूं,
तो वो बारिश हो रही है जिसे मैं तुम्हारे साथ देखना चाहती
थी,
वो बिजली कड़कने की आवाज सुनाई दे रही है जिसके ,
...शोर में मैं तुम्हारे साथ चुप बैठना चाहती थी
वो बून्दें जो इतने सालो से मुझे मेरे , लिए किसी के होने का
एहसास कराती थी...
आज वो तुम्हारी याद दिला रही है।
जानती हमेशा से थी..तुम मेरे लिए सही नहीं हो ,
पर क्या करें हर गल्ती को भी स्वीकार लेता ,ये दिल है ना ,
है।

किसी फिल्म में सुना था" ,आना तो पूरी तरह आना वरना ,
 "आना ही मत।
तुम न ही पूरी तरह ,न पूरी तरह आ पाए ,से जा पाए....
आज मौसम की पहली बारिश हैऔर अपने साथ तुम्हारी ,
...याद ले आई है
उम्मीद कर रही हूँ तो ये याद भी अपने ,जब ये लौटने लगे ,
साथ लेती जाए।

Routine

I have always hated the idea of routine.
As per my theories, it doesn't let people shine,
And as a person, who likes to change everything in a while,
always have derived myself to escape from one place to enter another,
I always had liked the idea of my name to be associated with different pursuits.

And now, I don't know how to tell you this;
To my amaze, I am not tired of seeing you every day,
I don't need any other escape than you,
I don't want any other change but you,
I don't need any door to leave and enter another,
Here I am, happily accepting the routine of being called as yours till eternity.

Let the anger go

We will talk again,
maybe you'll get me then
It is not you, I know
I will wait, let the anger go,

It's not you hitting
It's the anger biting,
will not leave you there
for the anger you wear,

Soft and caring inside
I will wait, let the anger get aside,
we will talk again,
Maybe you'll get me then

I will wait for you to see,
from my perspective, believe me,
It is not you, I know,
I will wait, let the anger go.

Tame the anger that slays
Keeping us part ways
I will put forth my point again,
It will not go in vain

We will talk again,
Maybe you'll get me then,
It's not you, I know,
I will wait, let the anger go.

About the Author

Sonia Bathla, a software engineer by profession, spent her childhood reading several fictional stories and with no time realised her love for words and thoughts.

Khayal, is her debut book inspired by the people around her and the feeling she relates with them.

www.ingramcontent.com/pod-product-compliance
Lightning Source LLC
Chambersburg PA
CBHW020133180726
47992CB00022B/2623